The Honey Bee

and the

Apple Tree

a Rosh Hashanah story

To Ayla & Eli,
Wishing you Sweetness.

The Honey Bee
and the
Apple Tree

a Rosh Hashanah story

Rabbi Joseph B. Meszler

Illustrated by KrisArt

PROSPECTIVE PRESS
Winston-Salem

Prospective Press llc

1959 Peace Haven Rd #246, Winston-Salem, NC 27106
www.prospectivepress.com

Published in the United States of America by Prospective Press LLC

 TRADEMARK

THE HONEY BEE AND THE APPLE TREE

Cover and interior art by KrisArt
© Prospective Press, 2021

ISBN 978-1-63516-003-1

ProP-G013

Printed in the United States of America
First Prospective Press hardcover printing, August, 2021

The text of this book is typeset in Powell Antique

To Joelle, who is the bee's knees

Once, a honey bee was looking
for a place to build a hive.

The honey bee saw a thick oak tree.

It flew up and asked, "May I build my hive in your branches?"

But the oak tree answered,
"I am too big and strong to be seen with little honey bees.
Buzz off."

 And the honey bee flew on.

The honey bee then saw a beautiful maple tree.

It flew up and asked, "May I build my hive in your branches?"

But the maple tree answered,
"I am too gorgeous to be seen with your
clashing yellow and black stripes.
Buzz off."

And the hurt honey bee flew on.

The honey bee then saw a tall elm tree.

It flew up and asked, "May I build my hive in your branches?"

But the elm tree answered,
"I am a wise old giant, and your flying
around is distracting my thoughts.
Buzz off."

And the very hurt honey bee flew on.

The honey bee then saw a small apple tree.

The apple tree was excited to have a visitor.

The honey bee flew down and asked,
"May I build my hive in your branches?"

And the apple tree kindly answered,
"That would be wonderful!"

They were very happy together.

Not too long after, God saw the honey bee's new hive in the apple tree's branches. The hive was dripping with golden honey, and the apple tree's red apples shone in the sun.

God said, "Better than being strong or beautiful or smart is to be kind. When people take apples from your tree and dip them in honey from your hive, they will remember that kindness is sweet."

And that is why the Jewish people dip apples into honey on Rosh Hashanah.

Rabbi Joseph B. Meszler is the spiritual leader of Temple Sinai in Sharon, MA, a noted Jewish educator, and a human rights activist. He is passionate about social justice and interfaith dialogue, fighting hunger and reducing gun violence. Rabbi Meszler has been a Brickner Fellow through the Religious Action Center of Reform Judaism, is a member of the Hevraya of the Institute for Jewish spirituality, and served as a Global Justice Fellow with American Jewish World Service in 2017-18.

Rabbi Meszler is the author of several books and many articles, including: *Gifts for the Poor: Moses Maimonides' Treatise on Tzedakah* (College of William & Mary 2003); *Witnesses to the One: the Spiritual History of the Sh'ma,* (Jewish Lights Publishing, 2006); *A Man's Responsibility: a Jewish Guide to Being a Son, a Partner in Marriage, a Father, and a Community Leader* (Jewish Lights, 2008); *Facing Illness, Finding God: How Judaism Can Help You and Caregivers Cope When Body or Spirit Fails* (Jewish Lights, 2010); and *Being Human (and Made in God's Image): Sermons on the Weekly Torah Portion, Jewish Holidays, & Topics of Today* (Kindle Direct Publishing, 2018).

CPSIA information can be obtained
at www.ICGtesting.com
Printed in the USA
LVHW071130090821
694898LV00002B/3